AF430021

Latter-day Grooks
2

From the Words and Wisdom of

Jeffrey R. Holland

Bill Wylson

Other Books by Bill Wylson

Latter-day Grooks 1

Hieroglyphs, Golden Plates & Typos

Give Place in Your Heart

Three Minutes Eighteen Seconds

Elder Hammond and The Inspector

A New Earth

The Manger on The Mantle

The Greatest Thing in The World

Available at:
billwylsonbooks.com

Author's Note: The grooks presented in this work are taken from the writings and teachings of Jeffrey R. Holland, Apostle of The Church of Jesus Christ of Latter-day Saints. I have attempted to cite sources from the published writings of Elder Holland; however, I have no authority or commission to speak in any official capacity for Elder Holland or for the Church.

The ideas expressed herein represent nothing more than the opinion of the author.

First Edition published September 2022
Second Edition published May 2024

Green Stem Media
White Horse Books
Salt Lake City, Utah 84009

*"If your life is a leaf
That the seasons tear off and condemn,
[He] will bind you with love
That is graceful and green as a stem."*
L. Cohen

www.billwylsonbooks.com
www.greenstemmedia.com

Table of Contents

For Dan Burke,
A good friend

An Introduction to Grooks

Many have tried to define what a grook essentially is. Most grooks say what any one of us may think ourselves, but they put pertinent new perspectives on everyday observations, presenting the reader with small instructions in the art of living.

Grooks were originally created by the Danish poet Piet Hein, (1905–1996) who wrote over 10,000 of them in both Danish and English. A grook ('gruk' in Danish) is a short aphoristic poem or rhyming aphorism. An aphorism is a concise, terse, laconic, or memorable expression of a general truth or principle. Aphorisms are often handed down by tradition from generation to generation. Literary experts suggest that the term 'gruk' is a compilation of the Danish words 'GRin and sUK', meaning to laugh and sigh, but Piet Hein said he felt that the word came to him out of thin air.

Hein was born in Copenhagen, Denmark. He studied at the Institute for

Theoretical Physics of the University of Copenhagen (later to become the Niels Bohr Institute), and Technical University of Denmark. Yale awarded him an honorary doctorate in 1972.

Hein's short poems, or gruks, first appeared in the daily newspaper *Politiken* in April 1940 shortly after the German occupation of Denmark when Hein was confronted with a dilemma. The Germans had recently occupied Denmark. Hein felt he had three choices; do nothing, flee to neutral Sweden, or join the Danish resistance movement. As he explained in 1968:

"Sweden was out because I am not Swedish, but Danish. I could not remain at home because, if I had, every knock at the door would have sent shivers up my spine. So, I joined the Resistance."

Hein's greatest weapon was his pen. His grooks were meant to be a spirit-building, coded form of passive resistance. The grooks are multi-faceted and characterized by irony, paradox, brevity, precise use of language, rhythm, and rhyme. They were often satiric in nature.

Hein's first grook passed the Nazi censors who did not grasp its true, hidden meaning:

CONSOLATION GROOK

Losing one glove
is certainly painful,
but nothing
compared to the pain
of losing one,
throwing away the other,
and finding
the first one again.

The Danes understood the deeper meaning and importance of Hein's grook and graffitied it all over the country. The hidden message was that even if you lose your freedom (i.e., losing one glove), do not lose your patriotism and self-respect by collaborating with the Nazis ('throwing away the other glove'), because betraying your country would be more painful when freedom had been won again.

Piet Hein was married four times and had five sons from his last three marriages. He died in his home in Funen, Denmark in 1996.

One of the author's favorite Piet Hein grooks is entitled:

VITA BREVIS

A lifetime
is more
than
sufficiently long
for people to get
what there is of it wrong.

In this volume, the author has attempted to cite the words and teachings of Elder Jeffrey R. Holland, an Apostle of the Church of Jesus Christ of Latter-day Saints and to express his ideas in the form of latter-day grooks.

A Message from the Author

As Latter-day Saints we understand that life is for learning. I have personally learned many life lessons over the years. These lessons did not always come easy. I made mistakes I hope never to repeat. Regardless, some of the mistakes were necessary. We cannot learn, change, and grow if we don't live life.

> *"I think in every lesson there's a blessing, and there's so many blessings from all the lessons I've had to go through in life."*
>
> *Alonzo Mourning*

There is so much to experience as we go about our daily lives. When we open our eyes in the morning, we never know what the day will bring—joy or sorrow, pleasure or pain, trials or triumphs—and this uncertainty certainly makes life interesting. It is a book of countless chapters, and we are the authors. We can daily look for opportunities to learn, grow and become more like our Savior. You never know where you'll find your next life lesson.

It is my sincere prayer that these messages of Elder Holland will offer insights into the lessons and experiences that God has established for our growth, benefit, and blessing.

"Keep thy father's commandment, and forsake not the law of thy mother:

"Bind them continually upon thine heart, and tie them about thy neck.

"When thou goest, it shall lead thee; when thou sleepest, it shall keep thee; and when thou awakest, it shall talk with thee."

Proverbs 6:20-22.

Green Stem
Media

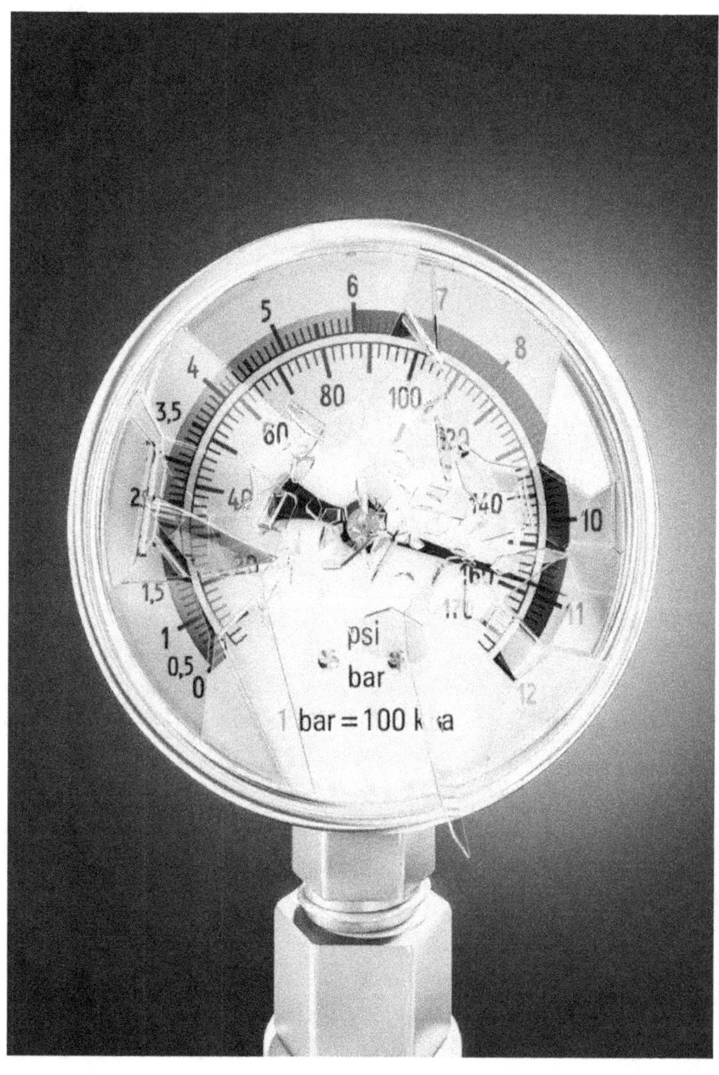

5
6
7
4
8
3,5
80
100
60
120
2
40
140
10
1,5
20
1
psi
0,5
bar
0
1 bar = 100 kPa
11
12

Under Pressure

Don't give up
When the pressure mounts.

Master your fears,
Face your doubts.

Blessings Come

Some blessings come soon,
some blessings come late,
and some don't come
till we pass Heaven's gate.

But for those who embrace
the Lord's gospel of grace,

    they come.

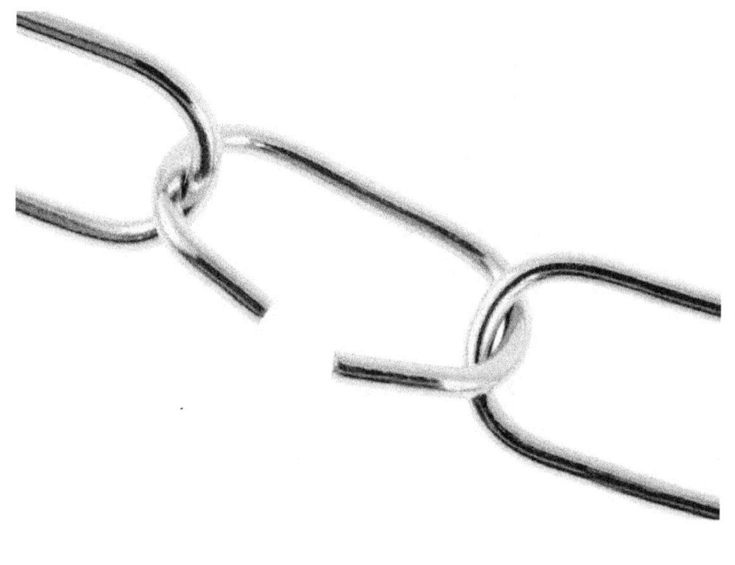

Making Repairs

Broken bones can heal and
broken hearts can heal but
so can a broken mind.

While God's busy
making those repairs

we can be helpful
by simply being merciful,
non-judgmental and kind.

Your Eternal Light

In a world that's grown
as dark as night,
where evil is
as evil does,

never forget
that Eternal light
placed in you
before this world was.

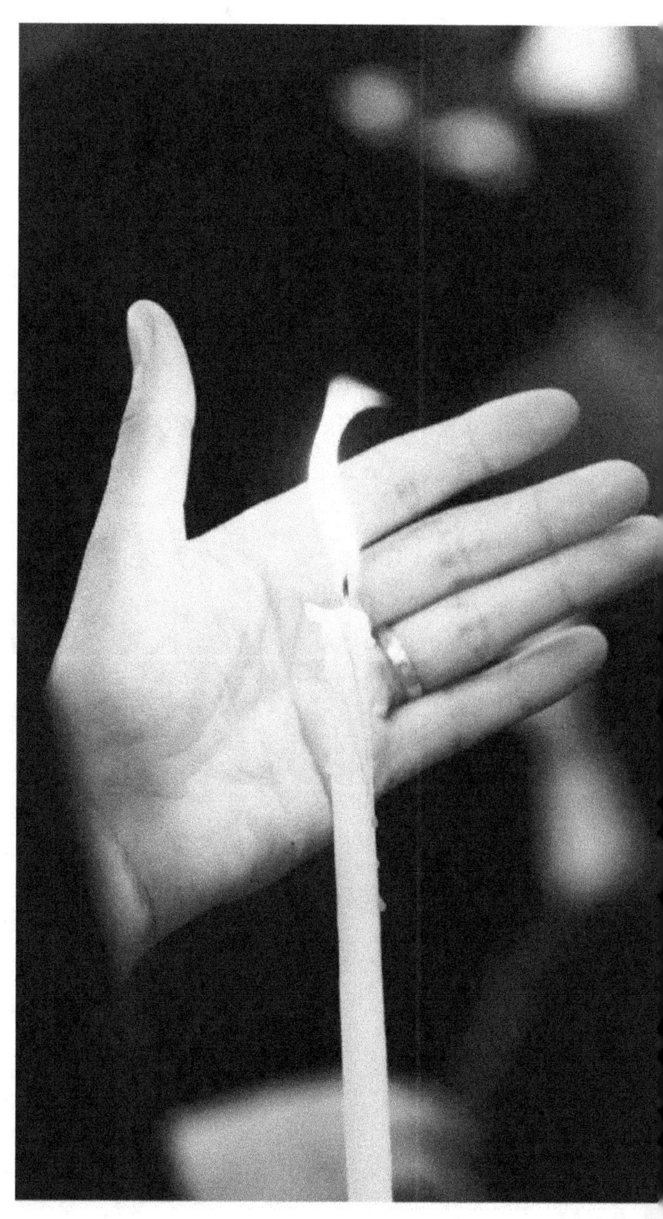

Lending Light

Bask in *His* light
then, without pause,
lend *your* candle
to the cause.

Longings of the Heart

When of us
difficult tasks are required,

even things our hearts
had not desired,

our loyalty
to the cause of Christ

is the supreme devotion
of our life.

"As the World Giveth"

In matters of
covenantal purity

(to any who walk
down that lane)

the sacred is often
made common

and the holy,
too often, profane.

Success
Sales
N
S
~40%
A   B
Plan
best idea
Time   Idea
Team
Success

Merciful Father

Above all else—
and it must be heaps—

that a divine being
has to do

He who never
slumbers nor sleeps

cares for the happiness
of me and you.

True Meaning

Through the incessant din
and drumbeat of our day,
may we strive to see

      Christ

at the center of our faith,
of our service,
and of our life.

The Temple is His House

Amid all the wonder
that we may encounter,

one purpose is instrumental:

We are to see, above
all else, the meaning of

Jesus in the temple.

HOLINESS TO THE LORD
THE HOUSE OF THE LORD

Uppermost In Our
Minds and Hearts

From the moment we read
the inscription
etched above the door—

the majestic doctrine
of Jesus Christ
should pervade our innermost core;

as it pervades the temple ordinances,
it should pervade our actual being

—right to the very last moment
we spend in that sacred building.

A Better World

Two divine directives
—to love God
and to love our neighbors—

are the only real hope

for granting our children
a far better world
than the one

with which they now cope.

Destiny

Our children
are the trustees,

(a truth that must
surely be faced,)

into whose hands
the destiny

of Christ's holy Church
will be placed.

Good News

At precisely the moment
when many are asking
deep questions of the soul,

we ought to be sharing
Christ's good news of caring
and inviting them into His fold.

The Bounty Giver

Begin your search for happiness
by making this simple shift:

Embrace the bounty
you *already* have

from the Giver of every good gift.

Don't Be Late

Occasional tardiness
is understandable

but when the situation
becomes too dire,

it's time to either
sell the ox

or, at least,
fill in the mire.

Spiritual Repair

Forgiving and forsaking offences
(the old and the new alike)

is central to the grandeur
of the Atonement of Jesus Christ

Practice Makes Perfect

We all have some habits
or personal flaws
keeping our spiritual
immersion at bay,

but God is exceptionally
good at forgiving…
perhaps 'cause we give him
so much practice each day.

Remember in a
Personal Way

Christ shouldered
alone, entirely,

the sins of
all humanity,

willingly
accepting His part

then He died
from a broken heart.

Self-Criticism

The grace of Christ
offers salvation
from sin and sorrow and death,

and it also
offers salvation
from persistent criticism of self.

Aspiring to Be

If we honestly
admit our faults,
and we honestly
try to improve 'em,

that does not mean
we are hypocrites,
it simply means
we are human.

Relationships

Indeed, to a great degree,
our relationship with Divinity

will be determined
or, at least, affected

by the 'least of these'
whom we've either

>   accepted
>   or rejected

Ministering

Just jump in
the pool and swim;

speed
toward those in need.

Don't dawdle and
please don't straddle,

deciding if you
should try to do

the backstroke or
the dog paddle.

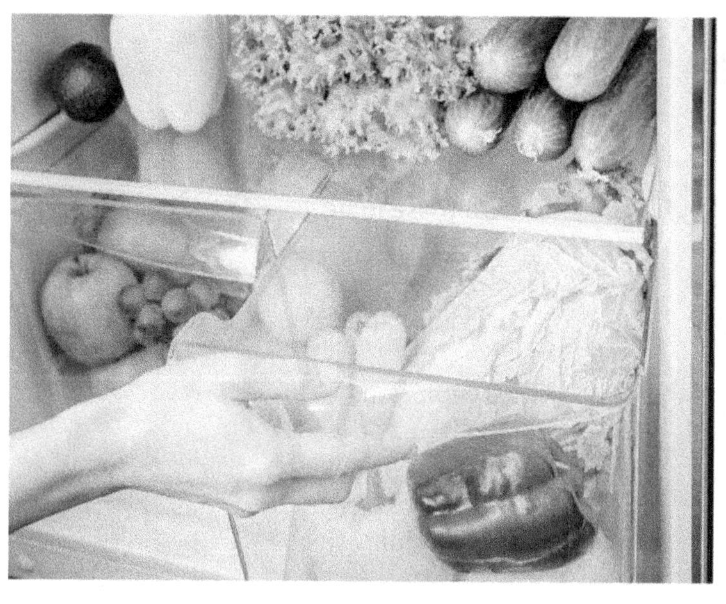

Old Grievances

Like the food in your refrigerator
whose freshness
causes you to speculate,

the old grievances stored
in your heart
have exceeded their expiration date.

Telestial, with a T

In a fallen world
where sin and
sadness are still trending,

our perfection
here in mortality
for now, at least, is still pending.

One Hundred Pence Perfection

If ten thousand talents
is too much to ask

be a bit more God-like
in the little tasks.

God's Choir

It is by divine design
not all voices are synergic—

it takes variety to make
God's rich celestial music.

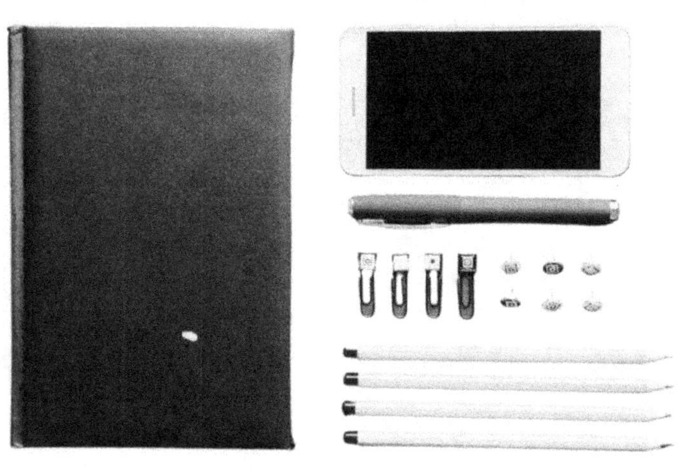

Excessive Expectation

Avoid the religion-ism
Of 'toxic perfection-ism'

Global Chorus

A great global chorus
will soon harmonize

across all racial
and ethnic lines.

The way is open
if you desire;

there is room for all
in God's global choir.

Chapter I
God loves You.

With All His Heart

The first great truth
of this universe—
in all this vast creation—

is that God loves you,

wholeheartedly,
without compromise,
and without *any* reservation.

A Happy People

If we love God
faithfully
He will give us
the ability

to love our
neighbor and then,
to also love
ourselves again.

Child of a Living God

You might want to run away
to places unfamiliar and far,

but never should you run away
from that person who you are.

Watch Peace Increase

When the love of God sets the tone
       for our lives
       and relationships and
       our feeling for all
humankind,

then old distinctions,
limiting labels,
and artificial divisions
       are easily left behind

       and then peace
       will increase.

Boom!

When our hearts acquaint
with the force of love
from God's heart,
      without restraint,

then that very hour
will bring a veritable
explosion of spiritual
      and moral power.

A Winding Path

When we pledge to follow Him,
our path will at times wind 'round,

by way of a stark Roman cross,
by way of a thorny crown.

Trust Until

Faith means trusting God
in good times and in bad
until we see his arm
revealed on our behalf.

Take Comfort

To those who follow Christ
there is one steadfast rule:

Christianity is comforting
but it's not often comfortable.

Here and Hereafter

The path to holiness
and happiness
here and hereafter
is a long and
sometimes rocky climb.

It takes time
and tenacity
to walk it, but
the reward is
monumentally sublime!

Beginning in the Grove

The most
important message
of the Restoration
is no deep mystery:

What was once
only hoped for
has now
become our history.

Heaven Help us!

With a cell phone in every hand,
we have morphed
the great command

from the Prophet's
personal stationary
of "every member a missionary"

to the underwhelming
moniker
of "every member a photographer."

Cry Out!

And if some days
our vision is limited
or our confidence has declined

And if some days
our strength is tested
and our belief is being refined

      —as surely it will be—

Then may we not fear or cower
but let us cry out all the louder,
"Jesus, thou son of David,

      have mercy on me."

Success

*"We thank you for following our
beloved prophet."*

If we stay aligned
with priesthood keys,
and follow the covenant trail,

and seek the Holy Spirit
to be our guide,
then surely, we cannot fail.

Healing the Past

Amidst the endless array
of old scars and sorrows,
the painful memories
  that mortality brings,

spiritual repair can come
from our divine Redeemer,
who rushes to our aid
  "with healing in his wings."

True Disciples

May we labor,
side by side,
with the Lord of the vineyard,
as our guide,

giving God our Father
a helping hand
with the staggering task
at His command

of providing comfort,
of answering pleas,
of drying tears, of
strengthening feeble knees.

Merciful Peacemaker

I am grateful that
God is a peacemaker
whose mercy will never cease,

because I am in need
of mercy and the world
is in need of peace.

God Can Bless

I am grateful that
God can bless
All those who
abhor or abuse Him,

because, without
ever wanting to,
sometimes, we *all*
despitefully use Him.

Perfect Love

I am grateful to know
God is perfect and that
He loves us endlessly,

because too often,
the "natural man"
can make us seem His enemy.

Except for Jesus...

No flawless performance
on this earthly stage
has ever been completed
in any age.

So, let's strive to improve
but not obsess
(with ourselves or others) over
expectations in excess.

Forgiven

I am grateful to know
that our God and Father
has a heart that is so forgiving,

because we all aspire
to a more Christlike life
than we often succeed in living.

When Joy Falters

In moments when
the melody of joy
falters below
your power of expression,

simply stand silent
and listen to others,
drawing strength from
their joyous accession.

Love Your Neighbor

The declarations of heaven cry out
as-a-matter-of-factly,

the only way complex societal issues
can ever be resolved satisfactorily

is by loving God and keeping His
commandments, exactly.

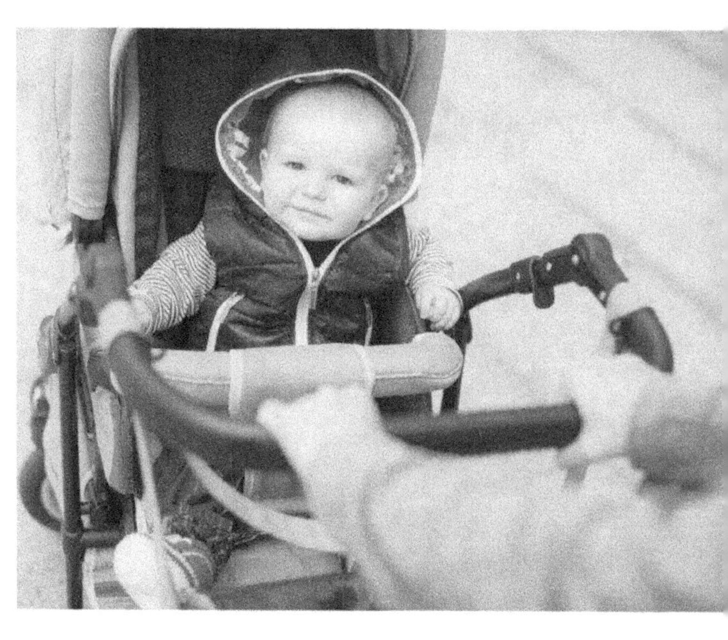

Punctuality

*"To those blessed mothers with
children and Cheerios and diaper
bags trailing in marvelous disarray,
who are lucky to have made it to
church at all."*

Fear not, and be
not disenchanted—

to you a late pass

will always be
lovingly granted.

Always Remember Him

Join the Great Physician
in His never-ending labor;

lift the load from the burdened,
relieve the pain of a neighbor.

At the Altar

May we bring *to*
the sacramental altar
"more tears for His sorrows
more pain at His grief."

May we take *from*
that sacred moment
"more patience in suffering,
more praise for relief."

Whatever Your Struggle

Trust in God.
Hold on in His love,
though the end you may not see.

One day dawn
will brightly break
and the shadows of mortality flee.

Will A Man Rob God?

Paying tithing is *not*
a token gift
we charitably bestow
on God in thrift.

Though some may not
believe it yet,
paying tithing is
discharging a debt.

Personal Purity

As the modern
winds of immorality
swirl luridly,

we have an obligation
of total chastity
and personal purity.

He Will Always Love Us

The first and great
commandment on earth
is to love God with all our heart each
day,

for surely the first great
promise from heaven
is that He will *always* love us that
way.

A Vital Message

Though you may feel
"like a broken vessel,"
and you're sure you can't hold water,

just remember
that broken vessel
is in the hands of a divine potter.

Live, Love & Hope

Until the hour when
Christ's consummate gift
is evident to us all,

may we live by faith,
hold fast to hope,
and let compassion be our call.

I hope you have enjoyed this little volume.

I would like it very much if you could post an honest 5-star review on Amazon or some other book site where you have an account and posting privileges. Maybe you can mention which Grook was your favorite.

If you found this book enjoyable, inspirational, educational, or enlightening, please tell your friends about it.

About the Author

Bill Wylson is the author of over 50 published writings on family values, religious issues, and religious education. His work has appeared in *The Ensign, This People, The New Era, Liberty Magazine, Success,* and others.

Bill graduated from the *Columbia School of Broadcasting* in Hollywood, CA as a commercial copywriter. He wrote trade journal ads for a major advertising agency in Los Angeles and public service announcements for a Los Angeles television station.

He has served as a volunteer Board Member of *Advocates of Single Parent Youth, Special Fun Games for the Disabled,* and on the Boards of Arts and Theater Councils. He has also served on Advisory Committees for the *Volunteer Center of Los Angeles* and on the *United Way Government Affairs Committee.*

Bill Wylson lives in Salt Lake City, Utah.

Other Books by Bill Wylson

Give Place in Your Heart:
31 Promises from the Book of Mormon

All of us are familiar with Moroni's promise that Christ will manifest the truth of the Book of Mormon to us by the power of the Holy Ghost. This is just one of many promises the Lord has made regarding the Book of Mormon.

In *Give Place in Your Heart*, Bill Wylson outlines 31 promises, with their attendant blessings and conditions, that the Lord would love to bestow upon you.

Climate change is real.

There really should be no question about it. However, polarized views about climate issues stretch from the causes and cures for climate change to issues of trust or skepticism in climate scientists and their research.

According to NASA: *"Climate change is one of the most complex issues facing us today. It involves many dimensions—science, economics, society, politics and moral and ethical questions—and is a global problem, felt on local scales, that will be around for decades and centuries to come."*

The only real question is: "What can we do about it?"

The answer might surprise you.

Three Minutes Eighteen Seconds:
A Prophet's Final Message to the World

Words are extremely powerful. Lord Byron poetically portrays this truth:

"But words are things, and a small drop of ink,
Falling like dew, upon a thought, produces
That which makes thousands, perhaps millions, think."

Three Minutes Eighteen Seconds examines three "small drops of ink" that are, simultaneously, extremely powerful words spoken by President Thomas S. Monson in the April 2017 General Conference, his final message to the people of this world.

Hieroglyphs, Golden Plates and Typos:

On the inside cover of his first leather-bound Book of Mormon, my father had written this quotation from the prophet Joseph Smith:

"I told the brethren that the Book of Mormon was the most correct of any book on earth, and the keystone of our religion, and a man would get nearer to God by abiding by its precepts, than by any other book."

Directly below this quote, my father had compiled a list of scriptures which he had labeled: "Mistakes in the Book of Mormon." Committing his writings to the future reader, Moroni candidly and apologetically acknowledged: *"And if there be faults they be the faults of a man. But behold, we know no fault."*

How did my father have the audacity to list mistakes in the Book of Mormon? To better understand these 'corrections' in the Book of Mormon and how they testify to its truthfulness and authenticity, we need to understand the process involved in making plates of ore and the method for inscribing on them.

Elder Hammond and the Inspector

"You know, there's a word to describe someone who won't even bother to meet his new companion at the bus station. It starts with an 'O' or, I don't know, maybe a 'C' or something. I think it's C-a—. No, I've lost it."

Elder Hammond was a freckled-face, shy sort of bumpkin from some rural farm town in Kansas. He was awkward and withdrawn. Even in his white shirt and tie he reminded you of the type of kid you'd see in denim coveralls, wearin' a straw hat and chompin' on a thin blade of grass whilst irrigatin' the lower forty.

I knew nothing about Elder Hammond's personal life. He was just a simple, quiet, humble boy, determined and dedicated. He had no delusions of grandeur, just a desire to serve. Perhaps more than any missionary, Elder Hammond had a purity of spirit and an altruistic motivation in ministering. I pitied him. I think he actually believed he could make a difference.

The Manger on the Mantle
A Christmas Tale based on Two True Stories

The Manger on the Mantle recounts the tragic life of Mark Spencer, a man raised in a small-town who somehow becomes very lost in the massive city of Los Angeles. He didn't become geographically lost; he became spiritually lost.

As his family falls apart and his world collapses, Mark begins to realize just how tainted his life has become. He has strayed so far from the innocence of his youth and now he fears he may never find his way back.

That's when Mark meets Marvin, a sockless, root-beer-float-toting ex-hippie. Together they journey the road to Bethlehem as they ponder the purpose of a birth that took place in a lowly manger.

The Manger on the Mantle is a beautiful story of hope and redemption and the joyous possibility of being given a second chance.

The Greatest Thing in the World
The Restored Gospel Version

In 1883, Henry Drummond, a Scottish scientist-evangelist, presented a powerful essay on 1st Corinthians 13, Paul's chapter on charity, the pure love of Christ. The "Restored Gospel Version" brings the added perspective of modern-day revelation to a timeless classic.

Drummond's message of charity is as vital and important today as when he first delivered it: *"The words which all of us shall one day hear sound not of theology, but of life, not of churches and saints but of the hungry and the poor, not of creeds and doctrines, but of shelter and clothing, not of Bibles and prayerbooks but of cups of cold water offered in the name of Christ."*

The Reverend Dwight Moody said that he had *"never heard anything so beautiful."*
The Greatest Thing in the World is a book that belongs in everyone's library.

References

A Gospel of Change — Gen. Conf. October 2013
A Holy Place — Gen. Conf. April 2021
A Message of Joy — Gen. Conf. April 2021
A New Normal — Gen. Conf. October 2020
A Priceless Possession — Gen. Conf. October 2016
A Time to Die — Gen. Conf. April 1992
A Vital Message — Gen. Conf. April 2021
An Invitation — Gen. Conf. April 2021
Are You Ready? — Gen. Conf. October 2020
Believe — Gen. Conf. April 2021
Better Than Ever — Ensign, January 2015
Bright Recollection — Gen. Conf. October 1990
Brimming with Joy — Gen. Conf. October 2016
Catch the Wave — Gen. Conf. April 2013
Choices — Gen. Conf. October 1990
Dying, We Live — Gen. Conf. April 1992
Faith Takes Work — Gen. Conf. April 2021
Focus — Gen. Conf. October 2016
Focus on Joy — Gen. Conf. October 2016
Gasping for Air — Gen. Conf. April 2017
Gathering Israel — Gen. Conf. April 2021
Greater Worth — Gen. Conf. October 2017
Hallmark — Gen. Conf. April 2018
"Hear Him" — Gen. Conf. April 2020
He Will Never Fail — Gen. Conf. April 2021
His Power — Gen. Conf. October 2021
Increase Your Faith — Gen. Conf. April 2021
It Takes Faith — Gen. Conf. April 2021

Kudos	Gen. Conf. October 2011
Let It Show	Gen. Conf. October 2013
Look Forward	Gen. Conf. October 2020
Making Time	Gen. Conf. October 2021
Move Forward	Gen. Conf. October 2020
Moving Along the Path	Gen. Conf. April 2019
Naturally	Gen. Conf. October 2012
Plague	Gen. Conf. October 2021
Pray from the Heart	Gen. Conf. April 2016
Riveted	Gen. Conf. April 2017
Roots	Gen. Conf. April 2004
Sacrifice	Gen. Conf. October 2018
Settlers	Gen. Conf. April 2016
Something a Little More Filling	Gen. Conf. April 1996
Spiritual Foundation	Gen. Conf. October 2021
Spiritual Shortages	Gen. Conf. April 1996
Steady Beat	Gen. Conf. October 2021
The Battle	Ensign, January 2015
The Joy of Redemption	Gen. Conf. April 2019
The Lord's Way	Gen. Conf. April 2015
The Pathway to Purity	Gen. Conf. April 2019
The Priesthood of God	Gen. Conf. April 2018
The Source	Gen. Conf. October 2016
This is Our Charge	Gen. Conf. April 2018
Truth is Truth!	Gen. Conf. April 2014
Unfailing Faith	Gen. Conf. April 2011
Unfinished Business	Gen. Conf. April 1992
We Show Our Love By Serving	Gen. Conf. April 2021
Where You Are Going	Gen. Conf. October 1990
Who You Are	Gen. Conf. October 1990
Why You Are Here	Gen. Conf. October 1990
Witness	Gen. Conf. April 2020

Green Stem
Media